BIG NUMBERS

AND PICTURES THAT SHOW JUST HOW BIG THEY ARE!

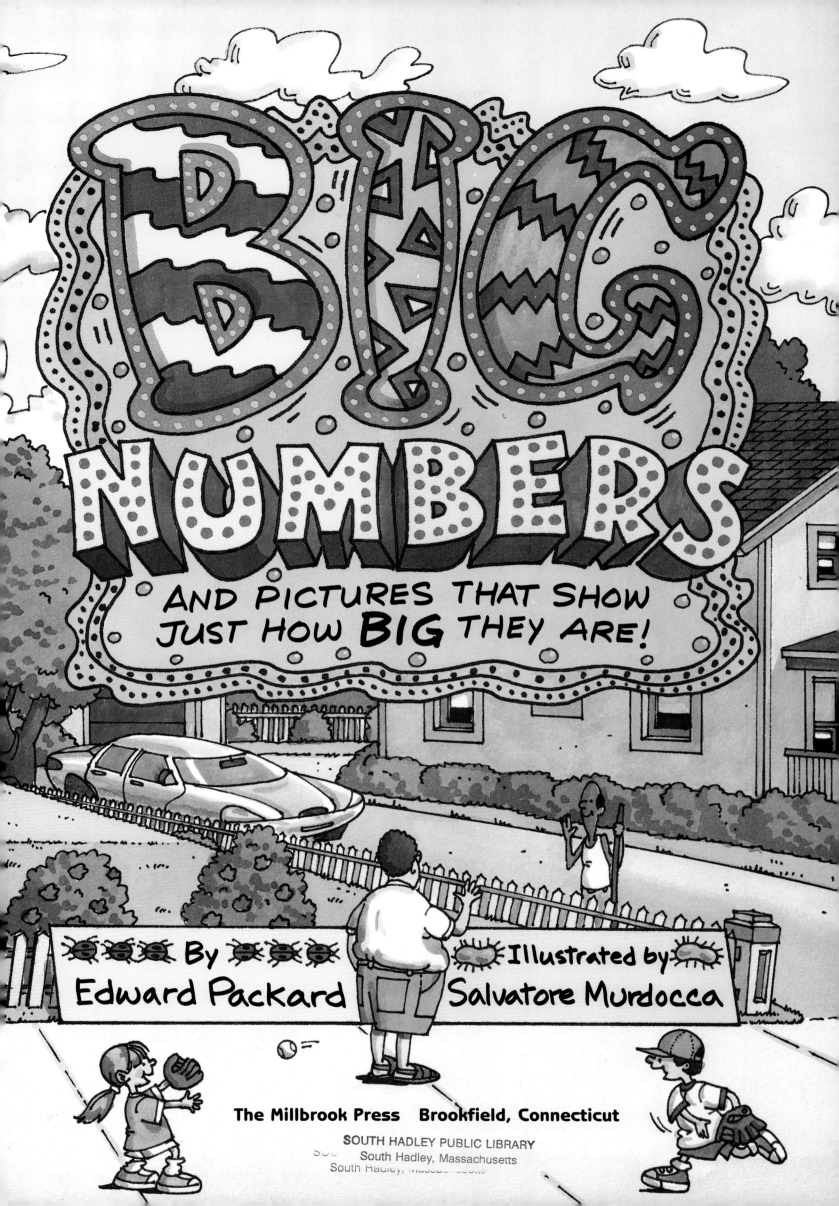

BIG BIG NUMBERS

AND PICTURES THAT SHOW JUST HOW **BIG** THEY ARE!

By
Edward Packard

Illustrated by
Salvatore Murdocca

The Millbrook Press   Brookfield, Connecticut

For
Amy,
David,
and Sam. — E.P.

To
my friend,
Victor. — S.M.

Library of Congress Cataloging-in-Publication Data

Big numbers : and pictures that show just how big they are! / by Edward Packard;
illustrated by Salvatore Murdocca.

p. cm.
Summary: Uses illustrations of exponentially increasing peas to present the concept
of numbers from one to a million, billion, trillion.
ISBN 0-7613-1570-5 (lib. bdg.) — ISBN 0-7613-1280-3 (trade)
1. Place value (Mathematics) Juvenile literature. 2. Decimal system Juvenile literature.
[1. Decimal system. 2. Exponents (Algebra) 3. Number systems.]
I. Murdocca, Sal, ill. II. Title.
QA141.35.P33 2000
513.5'5—dc21 99-32242 CIP

Published by The Millbrook Press, Inc.
2 Old New Milford Road
Brookfield, Connecticut 06804
www.millbrookpress.com

JUN 2000 J 513

You've seen big numbers, like

**a thousand
a million
and maybe even a billion**

How big are they?
How big can they get?

This book shows you.

SNIFF, SNIFF

We'll start small—with the number 1

ONE

1

One pea on a plate.

TEN

10

Ten is an important number because we have ten fingers and ten toes.

Ten peas on a plate.

ONE HUNDRED

100

Can you tell what month it will be a hundred days from now?

One hundred peas is a small helping of peas.

ONE THOUSAND

A thousand peas fill up a plate.

1,000

ARE YOU ME?

IN THREE YEARS.

In a thousand days you will be almost three years older than you are now.

TEN THOUSAND

It takes one hundred hundreds to make ten thousand.

10,000

YOUR FAVORITE.

AGAIN?

It would take a couple of months of eating a serving every day to eat ten thousand peas.

A million fleas in a row would stretch for a mile.

One hundred million peas fill up the kitchen and spill out into the dining room.

MILLION 10^8

100,000,000

A hundred million years ago a dinosaur might have been standing in your backyard.

ONE HUNDRED MILLION B.C.

WHERE DID YOU COME FROM?

IT'S A HUNDRED THOUSAND THOUSANDS.

OR 10^8

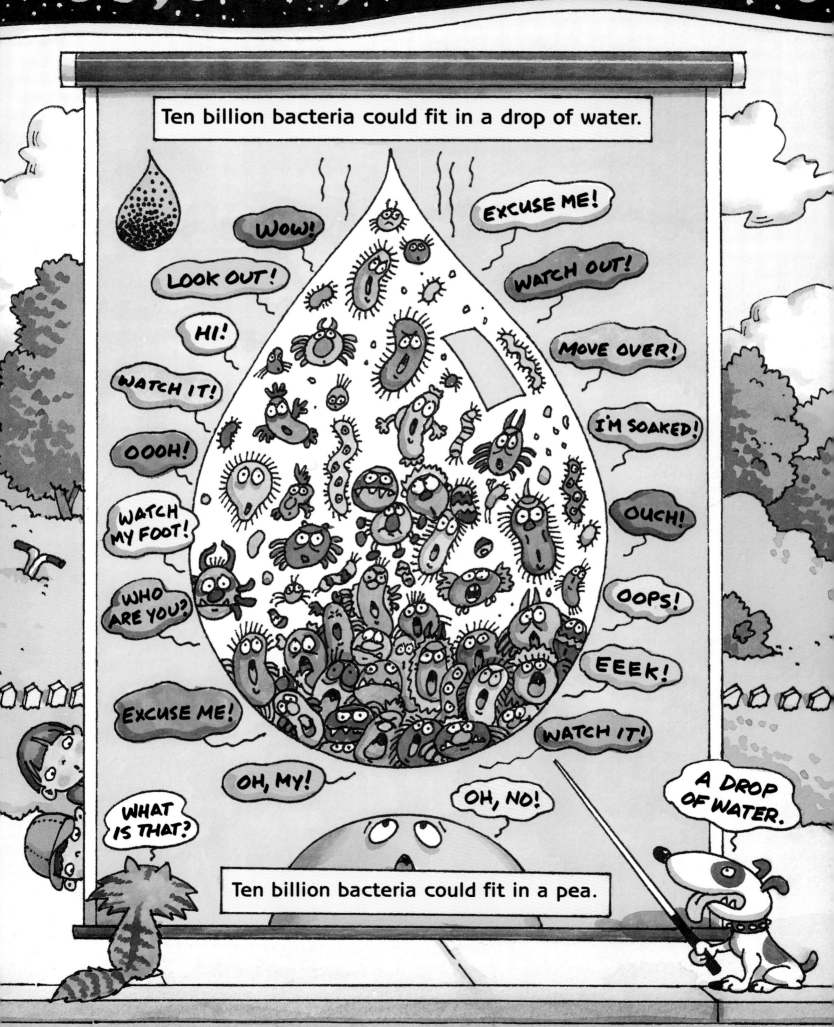

1,000,000,000,000

10^{12}

One trillion is a thousand billion.
One trillion is a billion thousand.

How big is a zillion?
Answer: A lot. But not a particular amount, because a zillion is not an actual number. Neither is a gazillion.

One quadrillion peas make a mountain!

"Infinity" means that to which there is no limit. And this is the symbol for it: ∞

No one can draw a picture of an infinite number of peas, because it would take an infinite quantity of paper and pencils to do so!

How could anyone tell how many peas would fill up a house, for example?

Here's one way. First count how many peas there are in a package of frozen peas. Then measure how much space a package of frozen peas takes up. Then find out how much space the average house takes up. Then figure out how many packages of frozen peas would fit in it. The number of peas that could fit in the house is the number of peas in a package times the number of packages that would fit in the house.

If there were a mountain of peas, wouldn't they get squashed down a lot by their own weight?

They certainly would. But to keep this book from getting too complicated, we imagined that all the peas stayed the same size.